Published in Great Britain in MMXX by
Book House, an imprint of
The Salariya Book Company Ltd
25 Marlborough Place, Brighton BN1 1UB
www.salariya.com

ISBN: 978-1-912904-77-8

© The Salariya Book Company Ltd MMXX
All rights reserved. No part of this publication may be reproduced, stored in or introduced into a retrieval system or transmitted in any form, or by any means (electronic, mechanical, photocopying, recording or otherwise) without the written permission of the publisher. Any person who does any unauthorised act in relation to this publication may be liable to criminal prosecution and civil claims for damages.

1 3 5 7 9 8 6 4 2

A CIP catalogue record for this book is available
from the British Library.

Printed and bound in China.

This book is sold subject to the conditions that it shall not, by way of trade or otherwise, be lent, resold, hired out, or otherwise circulated without the publisher's prior consent in any form or binding or cover other than that in which it is published and without similar condition being imposed on the subsequent purchaser.

Author: Roger Canavan
Illustrator: Damian Zain
Editor: Nick Pierce

Visit
www.salariya.com
for our online catalogue and
free fun stuff.

Kids in History
Albert Einstein

WRITTEN BY
ROGER CANAVAN

ILLUSTRATED BY
DAMIAN ZAIN

BOOK HOUSE
a SALARIYA imprint

• KIDS IN HISTORY •

$$(a+b)(o+b) - 4 \times \frac{1}{2}(6) \cdot (9)$$

$$E = mc2$$

$$a2 + b2 = ?$$

$$3 \times 2 + 4dy / 9 \ldots \infty$$

INTRODUCTION

Very few people, scientists or otherwise, have captured the public's imagination as much as Albert Einstein. How many times have you heard people say 'You don't have to be an Einstein' to understand something or other? He's often the first choice when people are asked to name a genius.

But calling someone a genius can make them seem impossible to understand because they're 'not like you or me'. We can learn a lot more about this particular genius by looking at his childhood. He can't have been discovering scientific wonders and promoting new theories as a toddler, could he? Learning about his childhood shows us something very surprising: he was a lot like you or me in many ways.

Like everyone, Albert found many things funny or scary or even difficult. No matter how many top marks he might get in physics or maths, for example, he still struggled to pass his exams in French. The sight and sound of soldiers marching in step terrified him as a child, which probably led to his life-long devotion to peace.

Then there are the parts of his life that give us hope, even if it's a little far-fetched. We've all gazed out of a window (even at school) and seemed to be daydreaming. Albert had a habit of doing just that, so much so that one teacher told him that he'd never amount to anything. Well, he did amount to something - changing the face of modern science and winning the Nobel Prize for Physics during a distinguished career. So maybe we can all hope that we'll amount to something...even when it looks as though we're not paying attention.

And even if we never reach those heights, we'll know that we still have a lot in common with a clever kid born all those years ago.

• KIDS IN HISTORY •

Chapter 1

Merchant Tradition

The southern German city of Ulm lies along the banks of Europe's longest river, the Danube. That riverside location made the city an ideal centre for trading in the Middle Ages. The first written mention of Ulm was in the year 854, nearly 1,200 years ago. That early settlement along the river grew larger and richer as merchants traded their cloth and leather goods with other European centres.

We can imagine what life was like during that time, with boatmen shouting and wagons taking goods to and from boats and barges. The smell of horse droppings and spilled beer would mingle with something much stronger - cow pee. Tanners, or people who produce leather, would soak animal skins in cow urine to soften them and to remove hair. Ulm must have been pretty smelly back then, as the tanners' workshops lined the river.

The air was sweeter by the 1870s, as the merchant Hermann Einstein and his wife Pauline went about their business. Ulm was still a busy trading centre, but the smelly tanneries had moved out of town and the people of Ulm earned their living from trading cloth, china and other goods. And the city was expanding far beyond its Medieval walls. As in other parts of Germany, new factories were springing up in the surrounding area.

Hermann Einstein and Pauline Koch were married in 1876, when Pauline was only eighteen. She had spent her childhood in Cannstatt, about 100 km north of Ulm. Her father was a successful grain merchant, so Pauline had a good education and the chance to become an accomplished pianist. Pauline moved to her husband's home city once they were married.

GET REAL

The country we know as Germany is surprisingly young, and was born in 1871 – just eight years before Albert Einstein. Before that the nation was divided into many large and small states. The people all spoke German and shared many customs, but the states were independent of each other. One of those states, Prussia, became very powerful in the nineteenth century, and in 1870 had defeated France in a war. It led the drive to unify Germany as a single country. The Prussian people valued discipline and military strength – two qualities that Albert would distrust all his life.

• KIDS IN HISTORY •

Like most first-time visitors to Ulm, she could have climbed the 768 steps of the steeple of Ulm Minster to marvel at the wonderful view. It was - and still is - the tallest church tower in the world. Pauline's artistic imagination would have taken flight high above the Medieval city. And along the distant horizon to the south she would have seen the snow-capped Alps.

Although Pauline would have been familiar with the church tower, she would not have worshipped in the church. Like her husband Hermann, she was Jewish. Ulm, like most German towns and cities, had a number of Jewish families involved with businesses and general trading. Being Jewish was important to Pauline and Hermann, even if they didn't go to the synagogue (Jewish place of worship) regularly.

GET REAL

Jewish people had been living in Germany for about 1,400 years before Albert Einstein was born in 1879. During that long period they had enjoyed periods of acceptance and peace – sometimes protected by Christian bishops – but also longer stretches of real hardship. Some Christians hated Jews and were envious of their success. Many Jews chose to leave Germany rather than continue to suffer. By the nineteenth century, German Jews found life easier but many of them took care not to stand out. Like many German Jews, the Einsteins were not very religious. But they took care to preserve many Jewish traditions, especially those that involved helping those in need.

Hermann's character was different from his wife's. Where Pauline was talkative and artistic - and sometimes used humour to mock people - Hermann was steadier and quiet. His background wasn't as comfortable as Pauline's, and he hadn't been able to afford university studies. But he was very interested in mathematics and engineering. Hermann was in business with his cousin. Together they ran a firm that sold bedding and mattresses.

We can see some of Hermann and Pauline's character in the Albert Einstein who would become a household name. Like Hermann, he was curious about how things worked - and why. And like his father, Albert would come to see mathematics as a beautiful language. But the spirit of Pauline also filled Albert's character. Like his mother, Albert would be witty, and at times even a little naughty, all through his life.

The world would have to wait to see these qualities develop in Albert Einstein. But in the meantime, on 14th March 1879, neighbours on Bahnhofstrasse B135, Ulm, were able to do a simple, happy sum: the Einstein family had just increased by one. Pauline had given birth to a baby boy.

Hermann, the proud father, went to register the baby's birth with the city officials in Ulm. He and Pauline had thought that Abraham would be a good name for a baby boy. But when Hermann arrived at the city hall, he had some concerns. While it was true that Hermann and Pauline had never suffered badly for being Jewish, who could say what lay ahead for their little boy? Hermann decided that Abraham sounded too Jewish, and that his son might be bullied because of his name and his background. So he decided on the name Albert. It was a popular name, partly because Prince Albert, a German prince, had married England's Queen Victoria. Albert was bound to grow up surrounded by other Alberts.

The arrival of baby Albert added yet more happiness to an already happy Einstein household. Because Pauline's family had more money than Hermann's, she was able to top up the money that

Hermann earned in the bedding business with his cousin. Hermann accepted this situation without feeling embarrassed because he appreciated his wife's generous spirit. In later years, Albert would observe how his parents' love for each other was a source of strength for the whole family.

• KIDS IN HISTORY •

A loving couple who were the proud parents of a baby boy, with steady (if a little unexciting) work in the bedding company, musical treats and occasional pastries - the Einsteins were happy in Ulm. We can wonder how Albert would have turned out if he spent the rest of his childhood in Ulm. But that wasn't to be, and there were changes around the corner... even if baby Albert was too young to understand.

• EINSTEIN •

• KIDS IN HISTORY •

Chapter 2
'THE DOPEY ONE'

Although the Einsteins were happy in their flat, with their small circle of friends in Ulm, Hermann began to feel that his talents were wasted selling mattresses and bedding. He was a responsible merchant, but his daily routine was far from the engineering problems that he really enjoyed solving. Some friends also felt that his kind nature was not ideal in the world of business. The family continued to make ends meet, but they were far from wealthy.

Hermann's younger brother Jakob, based in Munich, could see a different future for his brother. Like Hermann, Jakob loved maths and science, and he was a talented inventor. Unlike Hermann, Jakob had been able to study long enough to qualify as an engineer. There was another big difference between the brothers: their characters. Hermann was sweet natured and cautious, but Jakob was easily excited, and constantly trying out new ideas. Once he became caught up in a new idea, he would talk about it constantly, persuading others to join him.

Both Jakob and Hermann followed new scientific discoveries with interest, especially in the field of electricity. Over in America, the inventor Thomas Edison had demonstrated the first working electric light bulb in 1879 - the same year that Albert was born. Could that have been an omen for the future? Jakob believed that the brothers could become wealthy if they got involved in this exciting new field. After all, towns and cities across Germany - and Europe - were setting up electrical networks. Private houses and public buildings were being connected to these new electrical systems.

GET REAL

Apart from his first year in Ulm, Albert Einstein spent most of his childhood in Munich. With Germany still very young as a unified country, it was an exciting time to be in any German city. Munich was a special case, and it was proud of being the capital of Bavaria, a kingdom that had become part of the new Germany. The people of Munich were proud of the city's history and beautiful buildings. It attracted artists and musicians, which is why Pauline Einstein was happy there. And one of its most famous attractions was - and is - the Oktoberfest, a jolly festival celebrating local beer.

Ulm was still slow to 'go electric' so Jakob suggested that the brothers turn their attention to the largest city in southern Germany, Munich. Jakob already had a plumbing and gas-fitting company in Munich. By setting up an electric company there, the brothers could compete to get a very important contract - to provide electricity to the entire city.

Albert was just a baby when his uncle and father began to make big plans for their future in Munich. Pauline was pleased to see her husband so eager to improve their lives, but she also knew that the brothers would need to convince her as well.

The reason was money. Pauline knew exactly what Hermann earned, and how it was only just able to keep the family in their modest flat in Ulm. She also knew that Jakob, despite his excited talk about the future, was not wealthy. If a new business plan was to succeed, she would need to play a part, too. That's because of her dowry, the traditional gift that a bride's parents offer to a newly married couple. And because the Kochs were comfortably off, the dowry was generous.

GET REAL

Scientists and engineers had been experimenting with electricity since 1746, when the Dutch scientist Pieter van Musschenbroek developed the earliest method of storing and transporting an electrical charge. A breakthrough came in 1867, when the German engineer Ernst Werner von Siemens developed a powerful dynamo, or machine for generating electrical power. The Siemens dynamo produced electricity in a direct current (DC). Later electrical generators would use alternating current (AC), which made it easier to send the electricity over long distances.

Kids in History

EINSTEIN

It was generous, but not unlimited. Still, Pauline put her faith in the brother's plans and some of her dowry was put to use in the family's move to Munich... and later to build an electrical company. Baby Albert was only a year old when they moved to the 'big city' in the summer of 1880. Jakob moved in with the family.

Albert was still much too young to understand why his family had moved, or the excitement about electricity that his father and uncle shared. Instead, he was constantly in his mother's company, and it's more likely that he absorbed some of her loves. One of those was music, which could be heard coming from open windows as Pauline wheeled Albert through the Munich streets. And Pauline would play the piano whenever she had a chance, sometimes with her baby son napping nearby. In later years Albert would recall how much he enjoyed the way his mother played pieces by her favourite composer, Beethoven. Could the young genius have recognized Beethoven when he was just one year old? Maybe Albert was recalling some later performances!

The Einsteins had hardly settled in their new surroundings when another big change announced itself. Pauline was going to have another baby. And on 18th November 1881, she gave birth to a girl. They named her Maria, but everyone would come to know her by her nickname Maja.

Some of the first inklings of Albert's character date from that time. He was about two and a half years old and beginning to make sense of the world (and to speak). Some of Albert's first words after seeing his new sister tell us something about the person he would become. He looked down at the baby and then up at his parents and asked 'Does it have wheels?'

It seems that some of Hermann and Jakob's engineering qualities had rubbed off on Albert after all! But that funny sentence is memorable for another reason. Hermann and Pauline had become a little worried that their son was taking a long time to learn to talk. He would look at things, sometimes for a long time, and then... nothing. No questions or other comments. The Einsteins had a maid at that time, and she had a nickname for the little boy in the house: der Depperte, which is German for 'the dopey one'.

• EINSTEIN •

We know now that Albert was anything but dopey. But as he grew older, and perhaps all through his life, he would continue to 'test' words out. Looking back at their childhood, his sister Maja said: 'Every sentence he uttered, no matter how routine, he repeated to himself softly, moving his lips.'

Despite their worries about Albert's speech, Hermann and Pauline marvelled at how their little boy could concentrate. He would spend hours building things with his toy blocks, then rearranging them to make something slightly different. And all of that took place in silence as the little boy observed, moved a few blocks here and there, and then placed them in the new positions.

• Kids in History •

• KIDS IN HISTORY •

On warm days the sounds of the street would drift through the open windows of the Einstein flat in Munich. And Albert and his family would often hear the loud rhythm of boots marching in step. Soldiers in bright uniforms were a common sight in Munich and in other German cities.

• EINSTEIN •

Sometimes Hermann would take Albert down to the pavement to watch soldiers parade past. Brass bands played military marches and adults would cheer the soldiers. Other little boys would be looking on in astonishment, with excited expressions, and marching along the pavement in step. Albert would be the opposite: he would cry and clutch his father's hand, only settling once he was far from the upsetting noise.

• KIDS IN HISTORY •

Chapter 3
Off to School

Life in Munich provided a lot of opportunities for the Einstein family. Hermann and his brother Jakob continued to work together, taking on jobs that involved plumbing, but they spent more and more of their spare time developing skills with electricity. After all, the move from Ulm was based on Jakob's confidence that the brothers could make their mark - and become wealthy - in this new business area.

The electrical side of the Einstein brothers' business - building dynamos, lamps and measuring equipment - began to bring in money. They used some of it to build a house in the Munich suburb of Sendling. It was a quiet neighbourhood and the two children would soon discover that the garden could become their playground.

Pauline had adjusted easily to the move to Munich, perhaps because she had already moved recently - when she married - and she had fewer ties to Ulm than her husband. Munich was a wonderful centre for music, and she continued to play the piano. The family had enough money that Pauline could go out to lunchtime concerts while a hired maid looked after the two children.

Albert no longer wished that his little sister 'had wheels'. The small gap in their ages meant that Maja became Albert's closest friend. The two played together every day, and Maja looked up to her big brother - as she would for the rest of her life. According to his adoring sister, Albert was able to build towers from playing cards that were fourteen storeys high!

GET REAL

When five-year-old Albert was sick in bed one day, his father bought him a compass to cheer him up. What most of us see as a useful tool to find our way became something else to the little boy. He was so fascinated by the invisible 'magical' force that kept the needle pointing north, no matter how he moved the compass, that he trembled with excitement. Of course, what he had witnessed was the power of the force called magnetism. And magnetism is linked to the power of electricity, which was constantly being discussed by Hermann and Jakob. This fascination with unseen forces remained with Albert, and he later believed that this experience inspired some of his greatest scientific advances.

Perhaps that was a 'tall tale', but it does tell us a lot about Albert's ability to concentrate and to persevere with problems. That concentration would be stretched when he was five. Pauline bought Albert a violin and a music teacher came each week to give him lessons. Albert loved music, and his new instrument, but he was no lover of routine drills and practice.

Once Albert became so frustrated and angry that he threw a chair at his music teacher. The teacher fled the house, never to return. That story illustrates another side of Albert's character. Although he was able to concentrate for long periods, playing with the toy train that his uncle gave him or building things out of bricks and cards, he had a real temper. Poor Maja also became the target of hard objects being thrown around in anger.

• KIDS IN HISTORY •

Maja recalled what would happen when Albert exploded in one of his temper tantrums: 'At such moments his face would turn completely yellow, the tip of his nose snow-white, and he was no longer in control of himself.'

GET REAL

The patterns and repetitions of music are often compared to maths. Many musicians are good at maths, and many mathematicians and scientists enjoy music and play a musical instrument. Albert Einstein had influences in both areas – with his mother's love of music and his father's skill at maths. Music remained a particular love all his life, and many of his scientific ideas came to him while he played the violin. In later life, Albert looked back and said 'If I were not a physicist I would probably be a musician. I often think in music. I live my daydreams in music. I see my life in terms of music.'

• EINSTEIN •

This temper never flared up, though, on the walks that Hermann led into parks and woodlands on the outskirts of Munich. Both children loved how their father could identify trees and flowers. He would shush them to be very quiet so that the three of them could sneak up on red squirrels or nesting birds. As so often was the case, Albert was happy to listen and observe silently - and when they got home he would mimic the birdsong that they'd heard.

All this time Albert was preparing for another big change - he was approaching school age. At the time nearly every school was run by a major religion. That posed a problem for the Einsteins. Very few Jewish people lived in Munich, and the nearest Jewish school was on the far side of the city. Most people in Munich were Catholic, so the choice of Catholic schools was much wider.

Because the Einsteins valued their Jewish social ties - honouring traditions and behaving with kindness - more than weekly Jewish worship, they decided on sending six-year-old Albert to Petersschule, a good local primary school. It was run by the Catholic church. Albert was aware that he was different (being Jewish), but it didn't seem to bother him too much. Like the other pupils, Albert was taught about the Catholic faith, but thought of it as 'just another subject'.

The teachers at Albert's school treated him fairly and didn't single him out because he was Jewish. Albert even helped some of the slower learners in his class with their Catholic studies. At home he learned about Jewish customs and traditions. His parents weren't religious, but they wanted Albert to become familiar with his own culture.

Although Albert was rarely bullied by other

boys because of being a Jew, he did get his fair share of teasing and being roughed up. It was probably no worse than what anyone else faced, but Albert had a strong dislike of violence of any sort. It was that same feeling that caused him to be scared and uneasy when the German soldiers were marching by. As a result, Albert rarely went to friends' houses or joined in sports or other outings with the other pupils. He preferred to return home and lose himself in the projects that he always had on the go.

• KIDS IN HISTORY •

CHAPTER 4
THE YOUNG DAYDREAMER

Do you know what it's like to move from one school to another? Or from a junior school to a senior school? It can be pretty scary. And it must have been especially scary for Albert in October 1888, when he moved from his primary school up to Luitpold-Gymnasium, a senior school right in the heart of Munich.

GET REAL

Did Albert really have classes in a gymnasium? Yes and no, or at least not the sort of gymnasium that you might know. The word 'gymnasion' originally meant a place where young men in ancient Greece would meet for physical exercise as well as learning. Over time, some European languages (including English) dropped the idea of education from their understanding of the word. Other languages (including German) concentrated on the educational side. So Albert's gymnasium was really a place for bright pupils to prepare for university.

Everything about the new school was different from the smaller, welcoming primary school that Albert had been attending. For one thing, it was in the centre of a bustling city. And the size of the school - not just in numbers of pupils but of the building itself - seemed huge to the new pupil. The school uniforms seemed more formal, and even a bit like soldiers' outfits. It seemed that everywhere he went in the school he heard the word 'discipline' repeated. And that was never going to make Albert feel any more comfortable.

KIDS IN HISTORY

Even the sounds were harsh. Most of the people in southern Germany had a soft, easy-going accent. Some of the teachers at his new school, though, were from Prussia, the kingdom that was the real power in the new, united Germany. Prussian people were serious and keen on discipline and obedience. Their accent - to someone used to the softer southern German speech - seemed hard, and almost cruel.

The school believed that it was important to have a classical education. That meant understanding the great civilisations of ancient Greece and Rome. Albert would have loved to learn about how those ancient engineers had built the magnificent Greek temples and amphitheatres, or how the Romans could design something as huge as the Colosseum. Or perhaps they could learn more about the ideas of the great mathematicians, like Euclid, or scientists such as Archimedes. Instead, the lessons concentrated on dull repetition of Greek and Latin language lessons, which Albert found completely boring.

History was no better. The teachers were excited about their newly united country, Germany. They wanted to point out the glorious history of the German people that existed before the modern version of the country. That meant learning about the Holy Roman Empire. Despite its name, that Empire was mainly concentrated in German-speaking lands during the Middle Ages. The teachers would make the students memorise the names and reigns of the many Holy Roman Emperors. The trouble was that many of them had names that sounded alike. And if you weren't that interested at first - Albert certainly wasn't - it was easy to get those names confused.

Albert particularly mixed up Charles IV (1346–1378), Charles V (1519–1556) and Charles VI (1711–1740). The other pupils would find this funny, but not their teacher. More than once, he was told, 'Einstein, your presence in the class is disruptive and affects the other students. You will stay behind for detention.'

Life at home was a wonderful relief from the difficult atmosphere at school. Instead of facing harsh orders, dull parroting and strict discipline, Albert was able to live in his own world of puzzles and projects, also finding time to play in the garden with Maja. Music and laughter still featured in the Einstein household and the atmosphere was relaxed.

Hermann and Jakob had built a workshop, and concentrated on their projects. Albert was a welcome visitor and Jakob recognised that his young nephew had the intelligence and drive to understand some of their complicated work. At school, Albert and his classmates were still repeating their times tables over and over, with the teacher yelling at anyone who got them wrong or seemed bored.

One of the boys who often looked bored was Albert. He would often lose track of the repetitive classwork and gaze out through the window. No one would realise it, because he looked almost drowsy, but Albert would be working out complicated maths problems in his head or observing birds in flight or the way that the wind blew trees. Most of the teachers agreed with the history teacher who had assigned the detention: Albert was a lazy daydreamer. One teacher even said that Albert would never amount to anything in his life because he was so lazy.

EINSTEIN

Jakob was very different. He knew - and he knew that Albert knew - that instead of being dull and repetitive, maths could be fun. He began teaching Albert algebra years before it would come up in class. Many people find algebra difficult because it substitutes letters for numbers as it works out problems. Jakob took a different view.

'Algebra is a merry science,' he told Albert. 'We go hunting for a little animal whose name we don't know and call it x. When we bag our game we pounce on it and give it its right name.'

Albert remembered that clever explanation all his life. At the time, though, it especially pleased him to learn that other people could see maths and science in a different way, one that could be interesting and even amusing. In later life, when Albert was trying to explain some of his really complicated ideas to students, he asked them to imagine trains, trams and ships. He had remembered how his Uncle Jakob had helped him in the same way.

The challenge of a problem, which Albert often viewed as pictures in his mind's eye, captivated Albert. Maja knew that there would be times when her sometimes-playmate would be out of reach. Looking back at those childhood years she wrote, 'Play and playmates were forgotten. For days on end he sat alone, immersed in the search for a solution, not giving up before he had found it.'

One big difference between Albert's primary school and the Gymnasium centred on religious education (RE). Because Albert was one of the very few Jewish pupils at the first school, there was no Jewish RE. At the bigger school, though, Albert was part of a larger group of Jewish students. They had regular lessons concerning their religion.

Maybe because of those lessons or maybe because Albert was a bit unpredictable, he became very religious. His parents, who were not religious at all, were puzzled but didn't stop Albert from lighting candles, wearing prayer shawls and observing all of the many customs of the Jewish faith. He even composed hymns, which he sang as he walked to and from school.

• EINSTEIN •

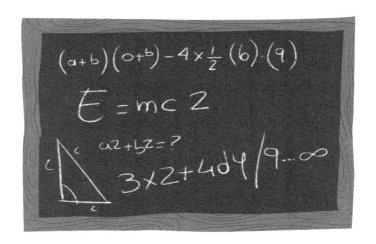

CHAPTER 5
SOAKING UP IDEAS

You have to be very stupid or silly not to recognise when someone is very intelligent. And although many of the teachers at the Gymnasium treated the school like a military camp - barking out orders and expecting obedience - some of them began to notice something special about Albert. In particular, he was showing himself to be very advanced in maths and science.

Hermann and Pauline never forced Albert to spend extra time on those subjects. They didn't need to - their son seemed to devour any books on the subject. His parents even became concerned about summer holidays, when there would be no school to channel Albert's growing interest in those subjects. Close to the end of each year they would buy him books on maths and science, so that Albert would be happily occupied during the time off from school in the summer.

Having Jakob around for maths discussions was also a plus for Albert. His uncle's playful instruction about algebra was still in the young boy's mind. He took a particular interest - while still only about ten - in geometry, the branch of maths that deals with shapes like squares, circles and triangles. Albert found triangles particularly interesting. Sometimes he would draw them out carefully and study them. Other times he would simply imagine them in his mind's eye (the way some teachers had mistakenly thought was daydreaming).

He showed his uncle a way to predict the length of certain triangles as long as you knew how big one of the three angles was. Jakob was astounded, because Albert had come up with the same conclusion as the great mathematician Pythagoras, who lived in Greece more than 2,400 years earlier.

That sort of mathematical study - at home and by himself - set Albert apart from other students. The maths teachers noted that at the start of each new school year, Albert would be totally familiar with the topics being discussed in maths class. That was hardly surprising: Albert had probably studied those topics and mastered them during the summer - or even the summer before! Another subject that captured his imagination was philosophy, the study of the most basic questions about human behaviour. In particular, Albert was interested in the work of Immanuel Kant, a German philosopher whose work explored the notions of space and time.

Around this time Albert found another source of inspiration, and it came from what might seem like an unlikely source. Hermann and

Pauline - unlike Albert, who had become very devout - hardly paid any attention to Jewish religious feasts and the faith's many rules about clothing and eating. More than once, Hermann described the Jewish religious rituals as 'ancient superstitions'. On the other hand, they were very proud of the accomplishments of Jewish people and the importance that Jews placed on kindness and charity.

One such tradition combined those two qualities. Jewish people were encouraged to be kind to - and help, if possible - 'scholars', or people whose lives were devoted to learning. With that in mind, Hermann and Pauline invited a poor young medical student to join them for dinner once a week. This was a Jewish custom that they were happy to follow.

• KIDS IN HISTORY •

The young lodger's name was Max Talmud, and he soon become a friend and guide for Albert. Together they would work out maths problems and discuss new scientific discoveries and theories. Max could see that Albert soaked

up information like a sponge and that he liked to read. He recommended a lot of books relating to science and maths, and Albert's parents were happy to buy them for their son.

It's a little scary to see some of the titles of these books in their original German. One of them was called *Kraft und Stoff*, which translates to *Force and Matter*. Hmmm. Other ten-year-olds were probably reading about cowboys and Indians and castles in their spare time. Here's another: *Kosmos - Entwurf einer physischen Weltbeschreibung*, or *Cosmos - Draft of a Physical Description of the World*. That's another book that no one else in the Gymnasium ever opened.

But the favourite of all the books that Max recommended was actually a series: *Naturwissenschaftliche Volksbücher* (*Scientific Popular Books*), by Aaron Bernstein. Those books took complicated and important scientific subjects and introduced them in an easily understood way. Many of the subjects were introduced as questions designed to capture the reader's interest. Albert found himself stopping to ponder questions like

'How much does the Earth weigh?', 'Can a ray of light be overtaken by something faster?' and 'Does the Earth rotate evenly?'

These subjects fascinated Albert. Just like Uncle Jakob, who could turn maths and science into stories, the Bernstein books fired the reader's imagination. Looking back at his childhood, the grown-up Albert recalled that he read those books 'with breathless attention.' Max and Albert discussed those questions, and sometimes Max would add a few questions of his own as he prepared to leave the Einsteins' house - knowing that Albert would spend the next week working out the answers.

Albert would wait for Max's arrival each Thursday, eager to share his new discoveries or the solutions to the problems that Max had set the week before. The *Scientific Popular Books* were the basis of these weekly problems. Max later remembered Albert's enthusiasm: 'After a short time, a few months, he had worked through the whole book. Soon the flight of his mathematical genius was so high that I could no longer follow.'

• EINSTEIN •

GET REAL

Albert was already fascinated by magnetic fields, and with his father's work with electricity. So it's no surprise that he wouldn't – and couldn't – let go of the image conjured up by Bernstein's question: 'What would it be like to ride with the electricity that flowed along telegraph wires?' Most ten-year-olds would have decided that the question was impossible to answer. Albert was different. The idea of speeding along on something that travelled at the speed of light got him thinking about something else that travels at the speed of light – light itself. Years later, as a world-famous scientist, Albert would ask his audiences to imagine travelling on a beam of light. With that image in mind, they might then find it easier to understand Einstein's Theory of Relativity.

Einstein

• KIDS IN HISTORY •

CHAPTER 6

A MIND OF HIS OWN

Concentrating more and more on his studies - mainly those he pursued at home - Albert spent less time with his younger sister. Maja remained devoted to Albert, as she would be all her life, but the two of them spent less time on nature walks with their father or simply playing in the garden.

Albert's closest friend, apart from Maja, at this point was certainly Max, who was only eleven years older than Albert and like a big brother to him. Max could see that his younger friend would overtake him and quite sensibly helped steer Albert towards areas where he could work on his own. It would be embarrassing for both of them if Albert began asking questions that were too difficult for Max. On one of his regular Thursday lunch visits he gave Albert a book on geometry, which gave detailed accounts of great mathematicians such as Pythagoras and Euclid.

It wasn't the first time that Albert had studied the work of those ancient mathematicians. And like before, he found that his own understanding grew the more he got to know their work. We can imagine Albert once more with that distant expression, gazing out through the window but in reality concentrating on what was going on inside his own head. And if the results of that concentration were complicated maths solutions, then Max could be proud... even if he no longer was the one guiding Albert's way forward.

Albert was never boastful about his ability to get to the root of complicated problems, or to devote himself to intense study. To his parents, he was still their 'little boy' who needed protection and affection, just like any other child. Max also saw that Albert had a gentle side that was very attractive. As a medical student, devoted to helping people overcome illness and injury, he shared Albert's dislike of the military nature of the new Germany. Max was born in Poland, so the German that he spoke was similar to the harsh accent of neighbouring Prussia. Albert's soft, southern German accent was a sort of reminder of the soft, kind personality of his talented young friend.

Something else began to stir in Albert's mind. Like many people with real curiosity, he looked for underlying reasons to explain why and how the world is the way it is. His devotion to Jewish religious customs reflected that search. His ancestors must have been right, he had observed, because the Bible tells us that they were. As a result, he had become very religious himself, much to his parents' surprise.

Candles, prayer shawl, prayer book and kippa (special Jewish cap) were all symbols of that devotion. And Albert's prayers and hymns had a special purpose for a boy of his age. They were preparing him for the sacred Jewish custom of Bar Mitzvah, the ceremony at which a boy becomes a man in the eyes of his fellow worshippers. But as Albert reached twelve, the normal age for a Bar Mitzvah, something very strange happened. And once again his parents were taken by surprise.

The Einsteins learned that Albert had given up his religious practices - and given up religion completely. At the Gymnasium he was still taking part in Jewish studies, so it's unlikely that his schooling turned him away from religion. In fact, right up to the moment that he gave up his beliefs, he had been impressed by the faith and courage of the Old Testament characters.

• EINSTEIN •

It's also unlikely that his beloved Bernstein books drove him away from belief. In fact, Bernstein wrote that there was - and should be - a natural balance between scientific knowledge and religious faith. It's most likely that Albert's belief (or lack of it) simply developed within himself, like so much of his beliefs and understanding.

GET REAL

Like many young people, Albert held strong opinions and defended them vigorously. If, some time later, he came to a completely different conclusion he would argue just the opposite. His about-turn with religion is a good example. Like many people, when he began to see things from a slightly different point of view, he abandoned the original ideas completely. In later life, he settled somewhere in between – not observing any religious ceremonies but concluding that natural laws can't explain everything, and that some force that we don't yet understand might be guiding it all.

The one book that might have helped push Albert away from Judaism was *Kraft und Stoff* (*Force and Matter*). Its author, Ludwig Büchner, disagreed with Bernstein and believed that actions here on Earth - and in the wider universe - all had natural causes. There was no place for religion in that kind of thinking. And it was a way of thinking that attracted Albert.

Referring to the Büchner book in later years Albert wrote: 'Through the reading of popular scientific books, I soon reached the conviction that much in the stories of the Bible could not be true.' He also felt that people in power did their best to trick people - especially young people - into believing such stories.

Being logical, Albert didn't stop with being suspicious about religion. 'Suspicion against every kind of authority grew out of this experience, an attitude which has never left me', he later recalled. He came to believe that young people were being tricked by the state (national government). The trickery, he felt, led to people's adopting harsh Prussian military attitudes. The sense of fear he had felt, holding his father's hand years before as soldiers marched past, had developed into intense dislike.

Watching a display of soldiers marching in step to the sound of drumbeats when he was younger, Albert burst into tears and told his parents, 'When I grow up, I don't want to be one of those poor people.' Now, that little bit older, he would be scornful: 'When a person can take pleasure in marching in step to a piece of music it is enough to make me despise him.'

Albert became more convinced that this 'marching in step' attitude was what drove education. Learning at his school was mechanical and repetitive, which 'seemed very much akin to the methods of the Prussian army, where a mechanical discipline was achieved by repeated execution of meaningless orders.'

Things had certainly changed with this maturing Albert. But would these new attitudes lead to trouble?

• KIDS IN HISTORY •

CHAPTER 7

FAMILY SEPARATION

Albert was gradually maturing into an intelligent, free-thinking young man. Certainly there were events that jolted him forward or in a new direction - his first sight of marching soldiers, playing with his compass, the companionship of Max Talmud - but these were more like nudges in the same direction. It was a case of steady progress, which even seemed unremarkable (to unobservant people).

The year 1894 was different, for Albert and for his whole family. It would involve big changes in work, income, schooling and even the country where the family would end up living. And the family itself would wind up separated. How did this all happen? Some of the events led to each other. Others seemed to come out of the blue. But there's no denying that it was a year that they would all remember.

School continued to be a mixture of high achievement and frustration for Albert. Most teachers are reasonably patient with a young student gazing out the window - as Albert would do in primary school. But when an older student looks bored (as Albert must have been very often), then teachers can take it personally. One of Albert's teachers even told him: 'your presence spoils the respect of the class for me'. Albert wondered whether that was just an outburst or a signal that the teacher would like to see him expelled. After all, 'the young Einstein boy' had made it clear that he did not like the school's emphasis on discipline and repetition.

But other matters, away from school, made 1894 even more disturbing. One of the most dramatic episodes concerned the family business. Ever since the family settled in Munich, and all through Albert's school years so far, the Einstein brothers' company had been a success. In 1885, before Albert had even started school, it had two hundred people working for it. In the same year it provided the first electric lights for Munich's famous Oktoberfest, a celebration that still draws thousands of people to the city each year.

The company's reputation had grown further over the next few years. It won an important contract to install electric lighting in Schwabing, a large suburb of Munich. The brothers had been able to use their experience in gas and electrics for that project. The system used gas motors to drive two large dynamos that Jakob had designed.

Jakob had also been busy with his inventions, receiving patents for electric lamps, meters and other technical equipment. The company seemed strong and the brothers decided to help it grow even further. That would need more money, but companies - like individuals - can borrow funds when they need to make improvements or invest in more equipment. They took out mortgages on their property. Those are loans that use property as security (or guarantee): if you can't pay back the loan, then the bank takes the house from you instead.

People (and companies) take out mortgages all the time, so the brothers didn't worry too much about what was, really, a gamble. Unfortunately for Hermann and Jakob, the gamble didn't pay off. They had depended on getting contracts for bigger jobs than the Schwabing project - providing lighting for central Munich and other districts. But those contracts went to rival companies, and the Einsteins found it hard to pay back their mortgages. (Pauline's dowry had been used up years before to help set up the company.)

The family was forced to give up their lovely home. Things were made even harder for them as they saw it being knocked down so that a block of flats could take its place. Hermann, Pauline, Maja and Jakob took a dramatic decision. They moved south to Italy, first to Milan and then to nearby Pavia. Some Italian business partners had said that Italy would be a good place to start their business up again. Plus, Pauline had some wealthy relatives in Genoa (another city in northern Italy). They had promised the Einsteins some money to build their business in Italy. Other members of Pauline's family, the Kochs, promised to send money from Germany.

What about Albert? He still had three years of school to go. His parents decided that he should remain in Munich to continue his studies at the Gymnasium. Hermann wanted Albert to qualify as an electrical engineer. He would stay with some distant relatives in the city. But it was important to finish his studies in order to gain a place at a good university.

Albert definitely wanted to go to university, but continuing at the Gymnasium suddenly looked a lot harder without the backing of his loving family and comfortable home. Things become a little confused as we investigate Albert's life at this time. Some people believe that he became very stressed and even had (what was called at the time) a 'nervous breakdown'. Others say that the staff at the Gymnasium thought it would be easier to get rid of this possible trouble-maker now that his family was no longer there to object. Albert was convinced that the teacher who had complained earlier about classroom respect was now 'out to get him'.

One thing we do know for sure is that Albert left his studies at the Gymnasium in December 1894. The time had come - in Albert's mind - to take some sort of dramatic action. He decided that enough was enough, and that he needed to leave the school. But he couldn't just walk away. Albert did what many people have done before and since - he got a sick note. He planned to use it to let him finish his studies at the Gymnasium.

• EINSTEIN •

A friend of Albert's, called Yuri, had understood Albert's problem. Yuri knew of a doctor in Munich who could help. The doctor wrote that Albert was suffering from a type of nervous exhaustion. He recommended that Albert stop his studies at the school and take a six-month break. Albert had the doctor's note in his pocket when he was summoned to the office of the headmaster at the Gymnasium. The headmaster told Albert that he must leave the school, so the medical proof didn't need to be presented. One of the maths teachers had known of Albert's plan to leave the Gymnasium. Unlike most of the teachers, he recognised Albert's special qualities. He told Albert, 'I knew you were going to leave the Gymnasium before you did.'

It's not hard to imagine where Albert decided to spend his time 'recovering'. He decided to join his family in Italy. Not only would it give him a chance to be with his parents, Maja and Uncle Jakob, it would be a delightful change from the dreary routine that he'd faced for years. Albert was excited about spending time in a country where the climate and people were warmer than in Germany. He was convinced that it was a place where scientific investigation could still go hand in hand with laughter and a love of music.

So in December 1894, Albert took the train south across the Alps and into Italy. He arrived at his surprised parents' doorstep determined never to return to study in Germany. His parents understood that Albert had been deeply unhappy. Although they were worried that Albert would end up with no qualifications, they wanted him to recover his spirits. So he remained with them in Pavia. During that time something very dramatic occurred: Albert Einstein wrote his first scientific paper.

The paper was given the title 'On the Investigation of the State of The Ether in A Magnetic Field'. Albert sent the paper to an uncle on his mother's side, Caesar Koch, who was surprised and delighted to read such a detailed study from a fifteen-year-old.

GET REAL

Is it surprising that Einstein's first scientific paper concerned magnetism? Perhaps it was a logical development of the same curiosity that he displayed a decade earlier, when he received the now-famous compass. Back then he was fascinated by the mysterious, invisible force of magnets. And now he was using his scientific skills to study that same force. In his letter to his uncle Caesar, Albert was modest about his letter-writing skills... but it was obvious that his real aim was to contribute to science:

'If you are not going to read this stuff I will not be annoyed at all; but at least you have to recognise it as a shy attempt to fight against my being a bad letter writer, which I inherited from both my beloved parents.'

Albert's stay in Italy couldn't last forever. Without proper qualifications he would find it almost impossible to get a good job. But the idea of returning to the Prussian attitudes of German education was too much for Albert to accept. Also, another big problem loomed. If Albert returned to Germany he would soon be forced (like other young men) to do military service. Being a German citizen was becoming a problem for the young man.

• KIDS IN HISTORY •

Chapter 8
An Imagination Takes Off

This happy period in the warmth of Italy couldn't last forever. Albert and his parents thought about the problems he faced and some possible solutions. He had dropped out of school, ruling out the chance of applying directly to a university. Going back to Germany seemed out of the question because of Albert's dislike of the educational methods there. Plus he would run the risk of being called up to join the German army very soon. Both of those prospects filled Albert with dread.

They decided that Switzerland could be the answer to those problems. German was the language of the educational system right through university level in Zurich, the country's largest city. It was even possible to sit the entrance exam for the Zurich Polytechnic (a university) without having completed school. And there was another advantage. Although Switzerland had an army to defend itself, the country remained neutral and was never involved in wars. That was very different from the aggressive military attitudes that Albert experienced in Germany, even in his school.

Albert made his way to Zurich to sit the entrance exams for the Polytechnic. Then something very unusual in Albert's life happened: he failed the exam! He had done well in the physics and mathematics sections, but failed biology, French and chemistry. The result was a shock, even though Albert had never been interested in - or tried very hard at - the subjects that he failed.

All was not lost, though. Albert could not be allowed to begin studies at the Polytechnic (because of the overall failure) but his maths results had been so good that the Polytechnic made him an offer. If Albert finished his formal schooling, he would be offered the chance to go to the Polytechnic. The director of the Polytechnic, who had been particularly impressed by the fantastic maths score, helped Albert secure a place at a secondary school in Aarau, a pretty town about 40 km west of Zurich.

Albert's unhappy memories of his recent schooling in Munich were still fresh, and he was disappointed at not going straight to the Polytechnic, so he was not very pleased about going 'back to school'.

Luckily, the experience turned into one of the happiest periods in Albert's life. The teaching at the Aarau school was very different from that of the Gymnasium. Teachers tried to keep their students interested the whole time. Many of them were happy to be considered friends of the students. Albert stayed with the family of one of those teachers, Jost Winteler. He was back living with a family, and a family with children about the same age as Albert.

Days at school passed pleasantly, with Albert soon realising that intense scientific study could be combined with companionship, and it could even be fun. Gone was the strict military-style discipline and tiresome memorising of facts that would soon be forgotten. Instead, students had lots of independence and freedom to devote themselves to subjects that interested them.

The school had a zoology museum with microscopes, and teachers encouraged the students to work independently in the science labs. Albert, of course, loved that side of learning. The school also appealed to other sides of Albert's character. Some of the other students were from families that had moved to Switzerland to escape hardship or cruelty in their own countries. Many of the senior students - those around Albert's age - spent their free time discussing social problems. Finally, Albert found himself in a setting where most people disapproved of wars and aggressive military displays.

And unlike his experiences in primary and secondary school in Munich, Albert made friends with some of the fellow students. The Winteler family remained welcoming and Albert enjoyed spending time with the Winteler children. They would often go for long walks in the nearby hills or make day-trips into Zurich. Maja would often visit and was drawn into the family just as much as her brother. In fact, Maja would go on to marry one of the Winteler children.

Albert was particularly interested in the fleet of trams that transported people around Zurich. Having lived so long in the company of engineers and electrical workers, Albert had developed a keen understanding of precision engineering. And the Zurich trams, especially the latest models with their fresh paint and attractive lettering, were excellent examples.

Some years later, while working in the Swiss patent office, Albert would produce one of the greatest works in the history of science: the Theory of Relativity. The theory was very complicated but Albert used some of the same techniques that his Uncle Jakob had used to teach algebra. Einstein would explain his theory by asking his audience to imagine themselves travelling on a tram. Those outings from Aarau to Zurich turned out to revolutionise the world's understanding of science!

Albert also called on those early memories of his uncle and his beloved first books to develop ideas that he could study. He would pose a question, like 'What would it be like to ride on a beam of light?', and then examine it from all angles. Much of that study would be conducted in his head, without the need to write anything down.

• Einstein •

• KIDS IN HISTORY •

GET REAL

We often think that scientific experiments call for complicated equipment and actions that are performed over and over again – and then compared with other actions. Only after such a process will the scientist consider the experiment complete. Albert Einstein would become famous for another type of experiment, known as a 'thought experiment'. He was always more at home imagining things in his head than writing them down on paper. That approach, which went back to his childhood 'daydreaming', would lead to some of the most important scientific breakthroughs of the twentieth century.

• EINSTEIN •

Chapter 9

Top of the Class

Life with the Winteler family - and at the school in Aarau - provided exactly the setting for Albert to begin to reach his full potential. Those around him, at school and at home with the Wintelers, recognised that he had enormous promise. The support generated real affection from Albert. Some lifelong friendships were forged in the classrooms, labs and dining halls of the school as well as at the Wintelers. Anna, one of the seven Winteler children, noted that Albert 'had a great sense of humour and could laugh heartily'. She commented on his intense studying but added that 'more often he would sit with the family around the table'. Albert's cousin Robert Koch also wound up staying with the Wintelers, arriving soon after Albert. The atmosphere became even merrier.

Maja wasn't the only young Einstein to form a romantic attachment with a Winteler. Marie, two years older than Albert, was his first love. In 1896 he wrote a note to his 'beloved sweetheart', saying 'I am no longer attracted to the girls who were supposed to have enchanted me so much in the past. You mean more to my soul than the whole world did before.'

Marie was also in love with Albert, who was by this point a very handsome young man. Although the pair would spend hours together playing music - she at the piano and Albert with his violin - Marie was aware of a major difference between them. Her parents were fond of Albert - and his parents even hoped for a marriage - but Marie sensed a real gulf in intelligence between them. She had completed a course at a teaching college in Aarau and hoped to teach in a local school, but she sensed that Albert's future lay far away, pursuing the most difficult scientific research. Their relationship didn't survive Albert's eventual departure.

Albert enjoyed the school very much, but some of the 'trouble subjects' continued to be problems. Jost would send Hermann Einstein reports of Albert's progress. He noted that Albert needed to brush up on his chemistry and that he needed private lessons in French. 'But', he added, 'with Albert I got used to finding mediocre grades along with very good ones, and I am therefore not disconsolate (unhappy) about them.'

Jost and Hermann also supported Albert when he renounced his German citizenship in 1896. That move freed Albert from the risk of being called up in the German army at any point. But for a few years he would remain 'stateless', or a citizen of no country. Albert did eventually become a Swiss citizen.

In late 1896 the time came for Albert to take the final exams that would decide whether he could enter the Zurich Polytechnic. First he had to take some exams at the school in Aarau. He got excellent marks in all subjects (except that troubling French) and came second in his school.

• KIDS IN HISTORY •

The Polytechnic exams turned out to be a real triumph. Albert got the top mark in maths, despite making a careless spelling mistake. He arrived late for the physics exam and left early, completing the two-hour test in an hour and fifteen minutes - and once more came out tops. Overall, Albert emerged top of his class even with another poor performance in French. But even that French exam essay announced his aim to devote himself to mathematics and physics.

Albert was about to take a step into a glorious future. His entry into the Zurich Polytechnic - and eventual world fame - was now guaranteed.

GET REAL

French wasn't Albert's strongest subject at any point in his schooling, but the French exam called for students to compose an essay in that language. Albert's effort was entitled 'My future projects'. It is fascinating; although it showed that he'd never become a professor of French it did give clues about the direction in which his enormous intelligence and creativity were leading him. Albert declared his interest in mathematics and physics. He modestly added, 'I suppose I will become a teacher in these fields of science, opting for the theoretical parts of these sciences.'

Kids in History

Einstein

• KIDS IN HISTORY •

CHAPTER 9

EPILOGUE

There's a special group of people who tower so high over their field that the world recognises them as geniuses. We're familiar with their faces even if we find it difficult to understand, or copy, their achievements. William Shakespeare, Marie Curie, Pablo Picasso and Nelson Mandela are among that special group. So is Albert Einstein.

Albert's eventual success in Switzerland saw him launched into a career that took him to the heights of scientific fame and achievement. Those achievements are marked on the Timeline on pages 138–143. His theories opened up new fields of study and changed the face of science forever. He travelled around the world, lecturing and teaching, but also held fast to his hatred of war and desire that scientific progress act to benefit mankind. It seems that the famous compass he received as a child also pointed the way to a brilliant future.

• EINSTEIN •

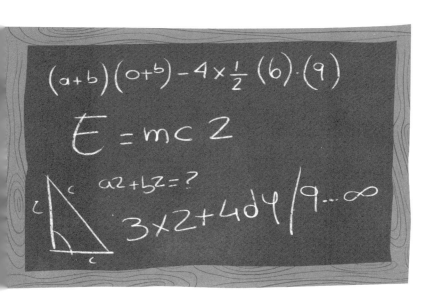

TIMELINE

1879 (14th March): Born in Ulm, southern Germany, to Hermann and Pauline Einstein.

1880: The family moves to Munich, where Hermann and his brother Jakob set up the electrical engineering company Einstein & Cie.

1881: Albert's sister Maria (nicknamed Maja) is born.

1884: Albert's father gives him a compass, which fascinates the five-year-old Albert because of the hidden force that moves its needle.

1885: Albert begins primary school at Petersschule, a Catholic school near the family home. He has Catholic RE lessons at school and Jewish lessons at home. He is the only Jewish schoolboy there.

1885: The first violin lessons for Albert – a teacher comes regularly to the Einstein home.

1888: Albert attends Luitpold Gymnasium, a secondary school in central Munich. The school has several Jewish students who join Albert for RE studies.

1889: Max Talmud, a young medical student, joins the Einstein family for regular meals and becomes a friend and guide to Albert.

1891: Albert becomes fascinated by a book on geometry, which he calls his 'holy book'.

1891: With the help of a rabbi, Albert becomes devoted to his Jewish faith and prepares for his Bar Mitzvah.

1892: Albert's increasing exposure to science drives him away from religion and he abandons plans for his Bar Mitzvah.

1894: Business problems force Hermann, Pauline and Maja to move to Milan, and then to Pavia in Italy. Albert is meant to remain in Munich to complete his schooling.

1894: Unhappy to be left behind, Albert finds

a way to leave the Gymnasium and follow his parents to Pavia.

1895: Albert tries to begin university studies at the Zurich Polytechnic but is unsuccessful as he fails the entrance exam.

1895: The Polytechnic recognises Albert's potential and recommends that he finish school in Aarau, near Zurich, and apply again.

1895: Albert moves into the house of Jost Winteler, one of his Aarau teachers. The Winteler family, with seven children, welcome their new guest.

1896: Albert gives up his German citizenship so that he will not be forced to join the German army. He becomes 'stateless' until 1901.

1896: Albert passes the Zurich Polytechnic exam as top of his class and begins his studies in October.

1899: Albert begins his application to become a Swiss citizen.

1900: Albert graduates from the Polytechnic with a teaching diploma in physics and mathematics.

1900: Albert fails to find a teaching post but submits a scientific paper to the Annals of Physics.

1901: The scientific paper is published and Albert is granted Swiss citizenship.

1902: Mileva Maric, Albert's girlfriend, gives birth to a daughter, Lieserl. Albert's father Hermann dies.

1902: Albert gets a job as a clerk at the Patent Office in Bern, the Swiss capital.

1903: Mileva and Albert marry, to the displeasure of both of their families.

1905: Albert's 'greatest year' sees four of his papers published in the Annals of Physics. These would change the face of science in the twentieth century.

1908: Albert is awarded a doctorate by the University of Bern.

1909: The job at the patent office ends as Albert becomes an associate professor of physics at the University of Zurich.

1910–1911: Albert works at the German University of Prague.

1914: After working briefly again in Zurich, Albert becomes a full professor at the University of Berlin.

1914: Albert signs the anti-war 'Manifesto to Europeans'.

1916: The General Theory of Relativity is published.

1919: Mileva and Albert, who had had two more children, divorce and Albert marries his cousin Elsa Löwenthal.

1920: Pauline, Albert's mother, dies.

1922: Albert is awarded the Nobel Prize for Physics.

1922–1933: Albert travels to many countries to lecture on his theories.

1933: Albert leaves Germany to escape the Nazis and moves to the United States. He takes a position at the Institute for Advanced Study, near Princeton University.

1939: As the Second World War begins, Albert writes to US President Roosevelt to urge research on producing an atomic bomb. Such a bomb could be produced using some of Einstein's theories.

1947: Albert works to promote disarmament, to prevent more world wars – or the use of atomic weapons.

1955: Albert Einstein dies in Princeton, New Jersey, USA.

• KIDS IN HISTORY •

WHO'S WHO

Caesar Koch (1854–1941): Albert Einstein's uncle on his mother's side. Was a businessman and merchant in Belgium. His interest in science led Albert to send him a scientific paper while still only fifteen.

Elsa Löwenthal (1876–1936): Albert Einstein's cousin and second wife. She was born Elsa Einstein and married Max Löwenthal, divorcing him in 1908. Married Albert Einstein in 1919.

Euclid (about 325 BC–265 BC): Greek mathematician, living in the Greek city of Alexandria (now in Egypt). Wrote extensively about mathematics and is considered to be the 'Father of Geometry'.

Hermann Einstein (1847–1902): Albert Einstein's father, a businessman who came to specialise in electrical technology. Business troubles forced him to move from Germany to Italy, where he formed companies with his brother Jakob.

Jakob Einstein (1850–1912): Hermann Einstein's younger brother. A qualified electrical engineer and inventor who was Hermann's business partner. His excitement about new projects outdid his ability to make them work as business ideas.

Jost Winteler (1846–1929): Swiss teacher of history and languages at the Aarau school near Zurich. His family welcomed Albert into their home as a guest while he studied at the school.

Ludwig Büchner (1824–1899): German scientist and author. His work *Kraft und Stoff* (*Force and Matter*) greatly influenced Albert Einstein as a student.

Maja Einstein (1881–1951): Albert's younger sister, known to her family as 'Maja'. Married Paul Winteler and eventually moved to Italy. Forced to leave Italy in 1939 because of anti-Jewish laws. Spent her last years near her brother Albert in the United States.

Max Talmud (1869–1941): Polish-born doctor and eye specialist who studied medicine in

Munich. He was a regular guest at the Einstein household, where he became friendly with ten-year-old Albert. He introduced Albert to many branches of science and was a great influence on his development.

Mileva Maric (1875–1948): Serbian physicist. Met Albert Einstein at the Zurich Polytechnic, where she was the only female student on the course. Had three children (one girl and two boys) with Einstein, marrying in 1903 but divorcing in 1919.

Pauline Einstein (1858–1920): Born Pauline Koch, was Albert's mother. Came from a wealthy family of grain merchants in Stuttgart. Most of her money was spent supporting Hermann and Jakob's businesses.

Pythagoras (about 570 BC–495 BC): Greek philosopher and mathematician. Responsible for many wide-ranging theories of philosophy but remembered especially for his mathematical study of geometry and triangles in particular.

GLOSSARY

Algebra A branch of mathematics that substitutes letters for unknown numbers as it works out solutions.

Bar Mitzvah A Jewish religious ceremony that marks a boy's passage into manhood at about the age of 12.

Dynamo A machine that produces electrical current.

Ether A material that people once believed filled the huge gaps between stars, planets and other objects in the universe.

Gymnasium The term in many European countries for a secondary school that prepares students for university.

Holy Roman Empire An empire consisting of a loose grouping of German and Italian states, lasting from the ninth century until 1806.

Manifesto A written statement of ideals or principles.

Matter All substances that take up space.

Medieval Referring to a period in European history, roughly from about AD 500 to 1500.

Mortgage A type of loan, usually to be paid back over a number of years, to help pay for a large purchase such as a house.

Nazis The name of a political party, led by Adolf Hitler, which took power in Germany in the 1930s and provoked the Second World War (1939–1945).

Nobel Prize An important annual award recognising excellence in many fields of study as well as honouring those who promote peace.

Oktoberfest A jolly festival held each autumn in Munich, attracting thousands of visitors.

Philosopher Someone who studies the nature of life, knowledge and truth.

Physics The science that deals with matter and energy and how they relate to each other.

Polytechnic A term used in several European countries to describe a university specialising in technical subjects such as science and engineering.

Prussia A region and former kingdom in northern Germany. It became powerful in the 1700s and led the way to unify Germany into a single country.

Relativity A complicated scientific theory that time and space are not constant, depend on each other.

Theory A set of rules that explains something.

Thought experiment A type of experiment that depends on thinking through possibilities rather than performing actions and observing them.

Tram A form of public transport that looks like a bus but runs on rails. Trams are often connected to overhead electrical wires in order to be powered.

INDEX

algebra 64, 71, 119, 147

Bar Mitzvah 90, 139, 147
Büchner, Ludwig 93, 144

dynamo 27, 40, 100, 147

Einstein, Hermann 10–11, 14, 16, 18–19, 23–24, 26, 32–33, 37, 39, 41, 45, 60, 70, 74–75, 101–102, 127–128, 138–139, 141, 144–145
Einstein, Jakob 24, 26, 30, 32, 39, 41, 60, 64–65, 71, 79, 100–101, 107, 119, 138, 144–145
Einstein, Maja 31, 33, 40–41, 43–44, 60, 65, 85–86, 101, 107, 119, 126, 138–139, 144
Einstein, Pauline 10–11, 14, 16–18, 25–26, 30–33, 40, 43, 70, 75, 101–102, 138–139, 142, 145
electricity 24–27, 30, 39–41, 82, 99–100
ether 108, 147
Euclid 59, 86, 145

gymnasium 53–54, 65, 69, 78, 90, 102–103, 107, 116, 139–140, 147

Holy Roman Empire 59, 147

Judaism 14–15, 18, 45, 48–49, 65–66, 75, 88, 90, 93, 138–139, 145, 147

Koch, Caesar 108, 110, 145

Löwenthal, Elsa 142, 145

Maric, Mileva 141–142, 146
Munich 24–26, 30, 36, 39–40, 45, 53, 99–102, 106, 115, 118, 138–139, 146, 148

Nobel Prize 7, 142, 148

philosophy 74, 146, 148
Prussia 11, 58, 88, 94–95, 111, 149
Pythagoras 71, 86, 146

Switzerland 114, 118, 136

Talmud, Max 76, 78–80, 87–88, 97, 139, 146
Theory of Relativity
trams 65, 119–120, 149

Ulm 9–14, 17–18, 20, 23, 25–26, 39–40, 138

Winteler, Jost 116, 127–128, 140, 146

Zurich Polytechnic 114–115, 128, 130–131, 140–141, 146

• KIDS IN HISTORY •